The Official

# NORWICH CITY FOOTBALL CLUB

## ANNUAL 2007

Written by James Bigg and Peter Rogers

A Grange Publication







ISBN 1 905426 44 5

£6.99

# CLUB HONOURS

## CLUB HONOURS & RECORDS

| | |
|---|---|
| YEAR FORMED: | 1902 |
| NICKNAME: | CANARIES |
| DIVISION THREE CHAMPIONS: | 1933-34 |
| DIVISION TWO CHAMPIONS: | 1971-72 & 1985-86 |
| DIVISION ONE CHAMPIONS: | 2003-04 |
| LEAGUE CUP WINNERS: | 1961-62 & 1984-85 |
| LEAGUE CUP RUNNERS-UP: | 1972-73 & 1974-75 |
| FIRST DIVISION PLAY-OFF FINALISTS: | 2001-2002 |
| FA CUP SEMI-FINALISTS: | 1958-59, 1988-89 & 1991-92 |
| UEFA CUP 3RD ROUND: | 1993-94 |
| BEST EVER LEAGUE POSITION: | 3RD IN PREMIERSHIP (1992-93) |
| RECORD WIN: | 10-2 V COVENTRY CITY MARCH 1930 |
| MOST GAMES: | KEVIN KEELAN 673 (1963-80) |
| MOST GOALS: | JOHNNY GAVIN 132 (1949-58) |
| MOST INTERNATIONAL APPEARANCES: | MARK BOWEN 35 FOR WALES (1987-96) |

# CONTENTS

JURGEN COLIN

# SEASON REVIEW

## AUGUST 2005

| | |
|---|---|
| NORWICH CITY 1–1 COVENTRY CITY | (ASHTON) |
| NORWICH CITY 1–1 CREWE | (McKENZIE) |
| NORWICH CITY 1–1 CRYSTAL PALACE | (ASHTON) |
| SOUTHAMPTON 1–0 NORWICH CITY | |
| MK DONS 0–1 NORWICH CITY | (McKENZIE) |
| NORWICH CITY 0–1 LEEDS UNITED | |
| STOKE CITY 3–1 NORWICH CITY | |

THE Canaries found themselves playing their first three league fixtures at home after their opening day opponents Coventry were forced to swap venues, with their new ground yet to be completed. Home advantage counted for little though, as City were held to a draw against the Sky Blues. Dean Ashton got Norwich off to the brightest of starts, heading home Dean Marney's cross on 21 minutes. But an unconvincing second half allowed Coventry back into the game and it was little surprise when Dele Adebola finished from close range on 65 minutes.

City were back at Carrow Road three days later for the visit of Crewe. It was the visitors who took a shock lead on 19 minutes, with Luke Varney producing a cool finish. Norwich – and particularly former Railwayman Ashton – wasted numerous chances to equalise before Leon McKenzie finally levelled things five minutes into the second half. It was one-way traffic after that, with Norwich laying siege to the visitors' goal but lacking that killer finish, allowing Crewe to escape with a point.

Norwich's hat-trick of home games was completed when fellow relegated side Crystal Palace rolled into Norfolk. Ashton got the Canaries off to a flying start with a close range volley on six minutes before England striker Andrew Johnson capitalised on some slack defending to equalise before the break. Ashton could have added to his tally in the second half, but his ferocious shot rebounded off a post, making it three draws in a row for Norwich.

Their first away match of the season ended in defeat, with Nigel Quashie scoring the winner for Southampton with a twice-taken penalty after Robert Green had saved his first effort. A Carling Cup game at MK Dons in midweek was only settled after a scrappy McKenzie goal in extra time.

Prior to the visit of Leeds United, the Canaries announced a new contract for star striker Dean Ashton, ending transfer speculation linking him with a move back to the Premiership. But despite the boost, City lost at home to Kevin Blackwell's side to a single goal from Robert Hulse.

A disappointing month was capped off at Stoke's Brittania Stadium with a 3-1 defeat – a game which also saw Darren Huckerby sent off for swearing at the referee.

# SEPTEMBER 2

| | |
|---|---|
| NORWICH CITY 2-0 PLYMOUTH | (DOUMBE OG, ASHTON) |
| WATFORD 2-1 NORWICH CITY | (LISBIE) |
| IPSWICH TOWN 0-1 NORWICH CITY | (HUCKERBY) |
| NORWICH CITY 2-0 NORTHAMPTON TOWN | (HUCKERBY, ASHTON) |
| NORWICH CITY 0-1 READING | |
| NORWICH CITY 2-1 HULL CITY | (SAFRI, DOHERTY) |

Norwich City got September off to the best possible start by recording their first league win of the season in front of the Sky television cameras at Carrow Road. Struggling Plymouth were the visitors, and the Canaries comfortably collected all three points thanks to a clumsy own goal by Doumbe before Dean Ashton added a second before the half time break to seal the points.

Unfortunately the Canaries got back to losing ways in midweek with a miserable trip to Watford. First half goals by Marlon King and Ashley Young put Adrian Boothroyd's side 2-0 up at the break. And although the Canaries battered the Hornets in the second half, they could only grab a single reply through Kevin Lisbie, who had joined on-loan from Charlton.

However, City spirits were soon lifted when a trip to Portman Road produced a memorable derby win over local rivals Ipswich Town. Norwich's cause was helped early on when Sito was red-carded for tugging back Lisbie as he homed-in on goal. The Canaries would then spurn countless chances to take the lead before substitute Darren Huckerby sealed the win with a coolly taken goal in the second half.

The Canaries returned to Carrow Road to face Northampton in the Carling Cup, and produced a workmanlike display to see off the lower league opposition thanks to a penalty from Huckerby and an instinctive finish from Ashton.

Norwich's league form continued to stutter though, as in-form Reading came to Norfolk to snatch a 1-0 win, with Ashton missing a last minute penalty to rub salt into the wound.

Norwich needed to bounce back quickly, and they did so in their next game by dispatching Hull City. The visitors took a surprise lead inside the first two minutes when defender Leon Cort headed in at the far post from a free kick. But a Youssef Safri-inspired Norwich were soon back in control of the match. Safri himself equalised with a trademark thunderbolt from the edge of the area before Gary Doherty grabbed his first goal of the season, heading in Dean Marney's pin-point right-wing cross. The Canaries could have helped themselves to more goals in the game, but poor finishing and fine goalkeeping kept the scoreline down.

SEASON REVIEW

## OCTOBER 20

| | |
|---|---|
| BRIGHTON 1–3 NORWICH CITY | (HUCKERBY, McVEIGH, HENDERSON) |
| NORWICH CITY 1–1 MILLWALL | (ASHTON) |
| LUTON 4–2 NORWICH CITY | (ASHTON, RYAN JARVIS) |
| QPR 3–0 NORWICH CITY | |
| BIRMINGHAM CITY 2–1 NORWICH CITY | (TAYLOR OG) |
| NORWICH CITY 0–1 SHEFFIELD WEDNESDAY | |

The Canaries finally registered their first back-to-back wins of the season by beating Brighton 3-1 at the Withdean Stadium. Darren Huckerby opened the scoring with a neat run and finish inside the far post before Paul McVeigh bundled in the second from close range. Frutos halved the deficit midway through the second half with a blistering long-range effort, but Ian Henderson made the points safe with 10 minutes left, curling in a delightful left-foot shot from just inside the area.

City returned to Carrow Road to face Millwall full of confidence but made hard work of the game. Adrian Williams gave the visitors the lead in the first half, with City equalising 10 minutes into the second period, Dean Ashton bundling the ball over the line after returning goalkeeper Andy Marshall flapped at a cross. But Marshall would have the last laugh, saving Huckerby's penalty before striker Barry Hayles was red-carded late in the game.

Things got even worse in midweek at Luton when Norwich found themselves 4-0 down inside the first 45 minutes. Norwich rallied well in the second half, with Ashton and Ryan Jarvis netting, but it was not enough.

That horror show was followed up by an equally disappointing display at QPR, where Norwich leaked three goals before the break without reply. This time there was to be no attempted comeback, with the Canaries returning from two away games empty handed and well beaten.

A break from the league came in the form of the Carling Cup, with Norwich travelling to struggling Premiership side Birmingham. The home side took the lead through Jermaine Pennant, but City equalised before the break when Blues' defender Taylor sent an Ashton cross into his own net. Norwich battled well second half, and it took an 85th minute pile-driver from on-loan Chelsea man Jiri Jarosik to put Birmingham into the next round of the competition.

A disappointing month for the Canaries was sealed at Carrow Road when Sheffield Wednesday became the latest side to take the points back home with them. Norwich were once again guilty of wasted chances against the Owls, and they were made to pay for lacking a ruthless edge when Chris Brunt scored the winner in the 79th minute to pile more misery onto City fans.

# NOVEMBER 2005

| | |
|---|---|
| NORWICH CITY 1-0 CARDIFF CITY | (ALEXANDER OG) |
| WOLVES 2-0 NORWICH CITY | |
| NORWICH CITY 2-0 LUTON TOWN | (HUGHES, HUCKERBY) |
| MILLWALL 1-0 NORWICH CITY | |
| COVENTRY CITY 2-2 NORWICH CITY | (DAVENPORT, FLEMING) |

Norwich returned to winning ways at Carrow Road against Cardiff. But again the Canaries were left needing a touch of fortune to claim the win, with the solitary goal coming in comical style with just 13 minutes left. Calum Davenport's header was blocked on the goal line by a defender, but it merely bounced back into the net off the back of goalkeeper Neil Alexander's head. All the same, a win was a win.

But Norwich failed to build on the result, stuttering to a 2-0 away defeat at Wolves where they barely mustered a shot on target.

Inconsistency was proving to be Norwich's biggest enemy so far, but they went some way to avenging their mauling at Kenilworth Road by seeing off Luton 2-0 at home. An early strike by Andy Hughes – his first for the Club – and a cool finish from Darren Huckerby earned a comfortable victory for the Canaries.

But their Jekyll and Hyde nature was to return in midweek as the Championship's bottom side Millwall grabbed a 1-0 win. City should really have been awarded a penalty in the second half, with the score at 0-0. But Huckerby's protests were ignored after he was floored in the box.

It was time for Norwich to show some true grit, and they did just that at Coventry City's new Ricoh Arena. With the score 2-0 to the home side after just 10 minutes, things looked very bleak for the Canaries. But a header from former Sky Blue defender Davenport just before half time reduced the arrears before Craig Fleming produced a cool finish with less than 10 minutes left to reward a good second half showing by the visitors. The game also marked the debut of midfielder Carl Robinson, who had arrived on loan from Sunderland. He would seal a permanent switch in January for £50,000.

# SEASON REVIEW

## DECEMBER 2005

| | |
|---|---|
| DERBY COUNTY 2-0 NORWICH CITY | |
| CREWE 1-2 NORWICH CITY | (McVEIGH 2) |
| NORWICH CITY 3-1 SOUTHAMPTON | (ASHTON 3) |
| SHEFFIELD UNITED 1-3 NORWICH CITY | (McVEIGH, ASHTON, MORGAN OG) |
| NORWICH CITY 2-1 BURNLEY | (CHARLTON, HUCKERBY) |
| LEICESTER CITY 0-1 NORWICH CITY | (McVEIGH) |

Norwich City's slump in form continued at the start of the month with a lacklustre 2-0 defeat at Derby. A Youssef Safri effort which slammed against the crossbar was the closest the Canaries came to scoring on a day when a brace from Andy Davies secured a comfortable win for the Rams.

It meant the pressure was on going into the game at Crewe, but City responded in magnificent style, recovering from being a goal down at the break to secure all three points thanks to a double from Paul McVeigh, his second coming five minutes from the end.

The win was followed by a memorable match with Southampton at Carrow Road when Dean Ashton became the first City player since Iwan Roberts in 2000 to bag a hat-trick. A rampant Norwich would have added more goals on the day but for the heroics of visiting 'keeper Antti Niemi who produced one of the performances of the season.

City kept up their winning run on Boxing Day by beating promotion chasers Sheffield United 3-1 at Bramall Lane. Phil Jagielka had headed the home side in front before McVeigh equalised before the break with a cool finish. Ashton then put the visitors ahead after the break before Chris Morgan's comical own goal sealed the Blades' first home defeat of the season.

Back at Carrow Road, the Canaries comfortably saw off Burnley thanks to a goal from Simon Charlton and Darren Huckerby before once again hitting the road for a New Year's Eve date at Leicester City's Walkers Stadium.

In a game which was far from pleasing on the eye, City grabbed their fifth successive win thanks to a late McVeigh effort created by a defence splitting pass from Dickson Etuhu. It was a great way to round off an excellent month, with manager Nigel Worthington collecting the Championship Manager of the Month title in the process. Their hopes of a play-off challenge had also been re-ignited.

# JANUARY 2006

| | |
|---|---|
| NORWICH CITY 0–3 PRESTON | |
| NORWICH CITY 1–2 WEST HAM UNITED | (McVEIGH) |
| PLYMOUTH 1–1 NORWICH CITY | (HUCKERBY) |
| NORWICH CITY 2–3 WATFORD | (McVEIGH, THORNE) |
| READING 4–0 NORWICH CITY | |

City's great run ended in spectacular style at Carrow Road when Preston left Norfolk with three goals and all three points. Adam Nowland put the visitors ahead in first half stoppage time before a second half penalty from Graham Alexander and a well-taken David Nugent goal sealed the win.

City were given a break from the league when Premiership new-boys West Ham came to Carrow Road in the FA Cup. With Dean Ashton out with a groin injury the Canaries were short of firepower and it was little surprise when the visitors took an early lead through Hayden Mullins. Marlon Harewood added a second before a penalty from Paul McVeigh reduced the arrears.

With the Canaries out of the FA Cup it was back to league action and a long away trip to Plymouth. Norwich secured a well-earned point thanks to a great individual goal from Darren Huckerby. The game was also the last in Norwich colours for Ashton. He limped off the pitch with a recurrence of his groin strain in the second half before completing a move to West Ham for £7.25m just over a week later.

Watford were the next visitors to Carrow Road and completed the double over the Canaries, twice coming from behind. A McVeigh penalty put City on their way and after Watford grabbed an equaliser it looked as if Peter Thorne's first goal for Norwich would seal the win in the second half. But the Hornets ensured there was a sting in the tail, with Darius Henderson equalising before Matthew Spring hit an injury time winner.

Prior to the trip to Reading, the Canaries announced the signing of West Brom hit-man and Welsh international Robert Earnshaw for a fee of £3.5m. Fulham defender Zesh Rehman and Charlton forward Jonatan Johansson also joined on loan, but their arrivals were not enough to prevent City from slumping to a 4-0 defeat at runaway Championship leaders Reading. That display and result left the Canaries a long way off the promotion chasing pack, with the play-offs now looking less and less likely.

# FEBRUARY 2006

| | |
|---|---|
| NORWICH CITY 1–2 IPSWICH TOWN | (JOHANSSON) |
| NORWICH CITY 1–1 HULL CITY | (DELANEY OG) |
| NORWICH CITY 3–0 BRIGHTON | (HUCKERBY, EARNSHAW 2) |
| NORWICH CITY 2–0 DERBY | (JOHANSSON, HUCKERBY) |
| CRYSTAL PALACE 4–1 NORWICH CITY | (WARD OG) |

Norwich's third defeat in a row came in the worst way possible with a derby defeat against Ipswich. Jonatan Johansson grabbed a goal on his home debut to put City in front before a deflected free kick from Jimmy Juan levelled matters before the break. The visitors had the better of the second half and with the clock counting down youngster Danny Haynes grabbed the winner, albeit with his hand. All the same, few could argue with the result.

Away at Hull it took an 87th minute own goal from home defender Delaney to secure a point for the Canaries before Norwich returned to winning ways at Carrow Road with a thumping 3-0 win over relegation-haunted Brighton.

Darren Huckerby gave City a first half lead before Robert Earnshaw grabbed his first goals for City with a brace in the dying minutes.

This was quickly followed up by a 2-0 home win over Derby County. Johansson scrambled in the opener before Huckerby sealed the points with a curling effort.

City might have been back to winning ways at home, but on their travels it remained a different story. And they finished the month in disappointing style with a 4-1 thrashing at Crystal Palace, with a Darren Ward own goal the only thing to show for their efforts on the day.

# MARCH 2006

| | |
|---|---|
| NORWICH CITY 2–1 STOKE CITY | (McKENZIE, JOHANSSON) |
| LEEDS UNITED 2–2 NORWICH CITY | (HUGHES, MCVEIGH) |
| NORWICH CITY 2–1 SHEFFIELD UNITED | (McKENZIE, EARNSHAW) |
| BURNLEY 2–0 NORWICH CITY | |

City returned to Carrow Road hunting a much-needed morale-boosting win, and that was exactly what they got in dramatic style against Stoke. The game looked to be heading towards a 1-1 draw after visiting striker Paul Gallagher had cancelled out Leon McKenzie's opening goal. But after some late heroics from Robert Green seemed to have preserved a point for the Canaries, super-sub Jonatan Johansson went straight up the other end to grab the winner.

A trip to in-form Leeds looked tough on paper, but City produced one of their best away displays of the season. Rob Hulse sent Leeds into the break a goal to the good, but Norwich came out all guns blazing and stormed into the lead thanks to goals from Andy Hughes and Paul McVeigh. City looked to be heading home with all the points until American international Eddie Lewis fired a free kick past Green for a cruel and undeserved equaliser with virtually the last kick of the game.

All the same, the performance meant Norwich were full of confidence as Sheffield United arrived at Carrow Road. And the Canaries completed an excellent double thanks to first half goals from McKenzie and Rob Earnshaw.

City fans then had to make a long Friday night trip to Burnley for a game shown live on Sky Sports. The Canaries looked well up for the match early on, with Johansson, McKenzie and Huckerby all wasting clear-cut chances. And they were made to pay as Andy Gray put the home side in front before the break with Graham Branch sealing the win early in the second half in a disappointing end to the month.

# APRIL 2006

| | |
|---|---|
| NORWICH CITY 2–1 LEICESTER CITY | (EARNSHAW, McKENZIE) |
| PRESTON 2–0 NORWICH CITY | |
| SHEFFIELD WEDNESDAY 1–0 NORWICH CITY | |
| NORWICH CITY 3–2 QPR | (HUCKERBY, EARNSHAW 2) |
| CARDIFF CITY 0–1 NORWICH CITY | (EARNSHAW) |
| NORWICH CITY 1–2 WOLVES | (EARNSHAW) |

City continued their excellent finish to the season at home with a win over Leicester. Rob Earnshaw latched onto a defence-splitting pass from Youssef Safri to put Norwich ahead before Gareth Williams equalised in the second half with a thunderbolt of a shot. It took a Leon McKenzie penalty to seal the win for City, who had now won their last five home games in a row.

But their away troubles continued at Preston as Norwich proved to be the architects of their own downfall. Own goals by defenders Jason Shackell and Gary Doherty sealed the win for the home side at Deepdale before losing again on the road to Sheffield Wednesday.

The game at Hillsborough saw a first start in goal for Paul Gallacher in place of Robert Green, who had injured himself in the warm-up.

And the Scottish international stole the show back at Carrow Road a few days later in a thrilling match against QPR. Gareth Ainsworth and Lee Cook had given the visitors a 2-0 lead midway through the second half and Norwich looked to be dead and buried. But this lead to a rousing fightback, with Darren Huckerby halving the deficit with a header with 12 minutes left. Gallacher then produced a stunning reflex stop to keep Norwich in the match before Earnshaw showed all his predatory skills to hit two in the final five minutes and seal an unlikely win for the Canaries.

Earnshaw was in hot form, and he showed it again when he returned to former club Cardiff. In a solid away performance it took a spectacular half-volley from Earnie to give City their first win on the road since New Year's Eve.

The result meant that Norwich would guarantee themselves seventh place in the Championship with a win over Wolves at home. Sadly, it was not to be, with Glenn Hoddle's side winning 2-1, with Earnshaw again on target for the Canaries as City ended the season in ninth place.

# APPEARANCES 2005 – 06

| Player Name | League | League Cup | FA Cup | Total |
|---|---|---|---|---|
| Robert Green | 42(-)- | 2(-) | 1(-)- | 45(-)- |
| Matthieu Louis-Jean | 2(-)- | - | - | 2(-)- |
| Adam Drury | 39(-)- | 1(-) | 1(-)- | 41(-)- |
| Jason Shackell | 16(1)- | 2(-)- | - | 18(1)- |
| Craig Fleming | 31(5)1 | 3(-)- | 1(-)- | 35(5)1 |
| Darren Huckerby | 39(4)8 | 2(-)1 | - | 41(4)9 |
| Jason Jarrett | 6(5)- | 2(1)- | 1(-)- | 9(6)- |
| Peter Thorne | 11(10)1 | 1(-) | 1(-)- | 13(10)1 |
| Dean Marney | 12(1)- | 2(-) | - | 14(1)- |
| Robert Earnshaw | 13(2)8 | - | - | 13(2)8 |
| Dean Ashton | 28(-)10 | 1(1)1 | - | 29(1)11 |
| Jim Brennan | 12(6)- | 3(-) | - | 15(6)- |
| Jonatan Johansson | 6(6)3 | - | - | 6(6)3 |
| Darren Ward | - | 1(-)- | 0(1)- | 1(1)- |
| Leon McKenzie | 11(9)4 | 1(-)1 | - | 12(9)5 |
| Youssef Safri | 25(5)1 | 1(1)- | - | 26(6)1 |
| Simon Charlton | 17(4)1 | 2(-)- | 1(-)- | 20(4)1 |
| Andy Hughes | 35(1)2 | 2(-)- | - | 37(1)2 |
| Paul McVeigh | 22(14)7 | 1(2)- | 1(-)1 | 24(16)8 |
| Zeshan Rehman | 5(-)- | - | - | 5(-)- |
| David Wright | 5(-)- | - | - | 5(-)- |
| Dickson Etuhu | 15(4)- | - | 1(-)- | 16(4)- |
| Paul Gallacher | 4(-)- | - | - | 4(-)- |
| Kevin Lisbie | 4(2)1 | - | - | 4(2)1 |
| Ian Henderson | 8(16)1 | 1(2)- | 1(-)- | 10(18)1 |
| Ryan Jarvis | 1(3)1 | 1(-)- | - | 2(3)1 |
| Jurgen Colin | 24(1)- | 1(-)- | - | 25(1)- |
| Rossi Jarvis | 0(3)- | 0(1)- | 1(-)- | 1(4)- |
| Calum Davenport | 14(1)1 | 1(-) | - | 15(1)1 |
| Gary Doherty | 39(3)1 | 2(1)- | 1(-)- | 42(4)1 |
| Michael Spillane | 2(-)- | [illegible] | 0(1)- | 2(1)- |
| Andrew Cave-Brown | 0(-)- | - | 0(1)- | 0(1)- |
| Carl Robinson | 18(4)- | [illegible] | - | 18(4)- |
| Own goals | 5 | 1 | - | 6 |

*Correct as at 02/05/2006*

# SEASON STATISTICS 2005-06

| | DATE | OPPONENT | RESULT |
|---|---|---|---|
| AUG | Sat, 6 | Coventry City | 1-1 |
| | Tue, 9 | Crewe Alexandra | 1-1 |
| | Sat, 13 | Crystal Palace | 1-1 |
| | Sat, 20 | Southampton | 0-1 |
| | Tue, 23 | MK Dons (Carling Cup) | 1-0 |
| | Sat, 27 | Leeds United | 0-1 |
| | Mon, 29 | Stoke City | 1-3 |
| SEP | Sat, 10 | Plymouth Argyle | 2-0 (OG) |
| | Tue, 13 | Watford | 1-2 |
| | Sun, 18 | Ipswich Town | 1-0 |
| | Tue, 20 | Northampton Town (Carling Cup) | 2-0 |
| | Sat, 24 | Reading | 0-1 |
| | Tue, 27 | Hull City | 2-1 |
| OCT | Sat, 1 | Brighton & Hove Albion | 3-1 |
| | Sat, 15 | Millwall | 1-1 |
| | Tue, 18 | Luton Town | 2-4 |
| | Sat, 22 | Queens Park Rangers | 0-3 |
| | Wed, 26 | Birmingham City (Carling Cup) | 1-2 (OG) |
| | Sat, 29 | Sheffield Wednesday | 0-1 |
| NOV | Tue, 1 | Cardiff City | 1-0 (OG) |
| | Sat, 5 | Wolverhampton Wanderers | 0-2 |
| | Sat, 19 | Luton Town | 2-0 |
| | Tue, 22 | Millwall | 0-1 |
| | Sat, 26 | Coventry City | 2-2 |
| DEC | Sat, 3 | Derby County | 0-2 |
| | Sat, 10 | Crewe Alexandra | 2-1 |
| | Sat, 17 | Southampton | 3-1 |
| | Mon, 26 | Sheffield United | 3-1 (OG) |
| | Wed, 28 | Burnley | 2-1 |
| | Sat, 31 | Leicester City | 1-0 |
| JAN | Mon, 2 | Preston North End | 0-3 |
| | Sat, 7 | West Ham United (FAC) | 1-2 |
| | Sat, 14 | Plymouth Argyle | 1-1 |
| | Sat, 21 | Watford | 2-3 |
| | Tue, 31 | Reading | 0-4 |
| FEB | Sun, 5 | Ipswich Town | 1-2 |
| | Sat, 11 | Hull City | 1-1(OG) |
| | Tue, 14 | Brighton & Hove Albion | 3-0 |
| | Sat, 18 | Derby County | 2-0 |
| | Sat, 25 | Crystal Palace | 1-4 (OG) |
| MAR | Sat, 4 | Stoke City | 2-1 |
| | Sat, 11 | Leeds United | 2-2 |
| | Sat, 18 | Sheffield United | 2-1 |
| | Fri, 24 | Burnley | 0-2 |
| APR | Sat, 1 | Leicester City | 2-1 |
| | Sat, 8 | Preston North End | 0-2 |
| | Sat, 15 | Sheffield Wednesday | 0-1 |
| | Mon, 17 | Queens Park Rangers | 3-2 |
| | Sat, 22 | Cardiff City | 1-0 |
| | Sun, 30 | Wolverhampton Wanderers | 1-2 |

| ATTENDANCE | % TURNOUT | POINTS | AWAY FANS | REFEREE |
|---:|---:|---:|---:|---|
| 25355 | 94 | 1 | 1385 | R. Beeby |
| 25116 | 93 | 2 | 243 | C. Penton |
| 25102 | 94 | 3 | 2100 | I. Williamson |
| 23498 | | 3 | 1723 | L. Probert |
| 4777 | | - | 1420 | A. Bates |
| 25015 | 95 | 3 | 1866 | U. Rennie |
| 14249 | | 3 | 1390 | M. Pike |
| 23981 | 91 | 6 | 663 | B. Knight |
| 13502 | | 6 | 1930 | P. Armstrong |
| 29184 | | 9 | 2300 | L. Mason |
| 16766 | | - | 1016 | C. Webster |
| 24850 | 95 | 9 | 986 | T. Kettle |
| 24740 | 90 | 12 | 854 | B. Curson |
| 6624 | | 15 | 750 | P. Joslin |
| 25095 | 95 | 16 | 1092 | P. Taylor |
| 10248 | | 16 | 1770 | S.Tanner |
| 15976 | | 16 | 2753 | R. Olivier |
| 28825 | | - | 1543 | M. Atkinson |
| 25393 | 93 | 16 | 1362 | J. Robinson |
| 23838 | 89 | 19 | 417 | D. Drysdale |
| 23808 | | 19 | 1036 | C. Foy |
| 25383 | 93 | 22 | 2337 | K. Wright |
| 7814 | | 22 | 953 | A. Woolmer |
| 20433 | | 23 | 2807 | R. Styles |
| 23346 | | 23 | 1522 | A. Hall |
| 6132 | | 26 | 857 | P. Joslin |
| 24836 | 92 | 29 | 848 | T. Bates |
| 26505 | | 32 | 1418 | T. Kettle |
| 25204 | 89 | 35 | 581 | C. Penton |
| 21072 | | 38 | 1864 | A. Leake |
| 25032 | 94 | 38 | 413 | N. Miller |
| 23968 | | | 3343 | M. Riley |
| 13906 | | 39 | 1142 | A. Penn |
| 25384 | 94 | 39 | 1405 | M. Atkinson |
| 21442 | | 39 | 1694 | L. Mason |
| 25402 | 97 | 39 | 2418 | K. Stroud |
| 20527 | | 40 | 2026 | J. Moss |
| 24038 | 86 | 43 | 505 | M. Thorpe |
| 24921 | 92 | 46 | 951 | A. Hall |
| 19066 | | 46 | 1282 | P. Walton |
| 24223 | 91 | 49 | 487 | P. Crossley |
| 24993 | | 50 | 1710 | C. Foy |
| 25346 | 92 | 53 | 2328 | P. Taylor |
| 11938 | | 53 | 515 | C. Webster |
| 24718 | 91 | 56 | 1731 | A. D'Urso |
| 15714 | | 56 | 933 | M. Fletcher |
| 30755 | | 56 | 2292 | K. Stroud |
| 24126 | 87 | 59 | 1172 | B. Curson |
| 11590 | | 62 | 624 | A. Marriner |
| 24081 | 90 | 62 | 982 | I. Williamson |

PLAYER OF THE YEAR 2005-06

# GARY DOHERTY

***He's known as the Ginger Pele – and last season Gary Doherty proved why as he walked off with the Barry Butler Memorial Trophy as the Canaries' player of the year.***

It was an award well deserved by the former Tottenham man after a huge number of consistent displays at the heart of Norwich's defence.

The 26-year-old Republic of Ireland international had a mixed first season for the Canaries after joining from White Hart Lane.

Often deployed as a striker, the Doc found it hard to secure a permanent first-team place in the side, struggling for fitness at the same time.

But Gary didn't rest on his laurels. He returned to pre-season several pounds lighter and ended up as one of the most consistent performers in the side.

And the Doc said picking up the player of the year award at the end of the season capped off a terrific personal campaign for him.

"It meant an awful lot to me," he said. "I was absolutely over the moon to be honest. It is very important that the fans respect you and think you have done a great job.

"I was in and out of the team and playing in different positions previously, but last year I have had a pretty rock solid season. I have played at the back most of the season and I think that has helped me a lot."

And Gary said his summer fitness regime helped him to get in shape and be best prepared for the rigours of Championship football.

"I worked quite hard towards the end of the previous season and very hard in the summer – and that is something I need to keep doing," he said, adding that continuity was the key to success for the Canaries in the future.

"We need to stop conceding goals," he said. "I think we conceded far too many last season and that might have come with the defence changing rather a lot. It's difficult to get to know each other's game – that is the main thing, continuity; the same players playing week in and week out."

The Doc played 42 times for the Canaries last season after a difficult opening spell where he found himself dropped from the side.

But he came back with a bang, most notably in the 1-0 win at Ipswich in September when his raking pass set-up Darren Huckerby for the winning goal.

The Doc began his career as a youngster at Luton Town. It was there he caught the eye of bigger clubs, thanks to his ability to play both as a defender and as a target man.

A move to Tottenham beckoned at the end of the 1999 season, but Gary found it hard to nail down a regular place in the first team at White Hart Lane. He spent four seasons with Spurs before City boss Nigel Worthington rode to his rescue at the start of the 2004 season, with Norwich newly promoted to the Premiership.

He made his debut a few days later in the match at Old Trafford against Manchester United, coming on as a second half substitute. His arrival was not enough to prevent Norwich from slipping to an unlucky 2-1 defeat.

But the following week his fortunes would change, with the Doc bagging his first-ever goal for City in the scintillating 2-2 comeback at Newcastle.

Fast becoming a cult hero at Carrow Road, the Doc will be looking to build on his excellent renaissance from last season and become a Norwich City regular for many years to come.

# SUMMER SIGNING

Speedy winger Lee Croft joined the Canaries from Manchester City in July and became Nigel Worthington's first signing of the summer. The 21-year-old signed a three-year deal at Carrow Road, despite being offered more money by a number of other Championship clubs.

"I spoke to other clubs, but when I came here for the first time my mind was more or less made up," he said on the day of his signing.

"I did speak to other clubs and I even told the manager that I got offered more money elsewhere as well, but it was a pure footballing decision and that is how I felt when I came down to the club and they made me feel so welcome. I am just looking forward to starting."

Croft is friends with fellow Canaries Dickson Etuhu and Darren Huckerby from their time at Manchester City and said he didn't feel the move away from the Premiership was a step-down.

"I didn't see it that way because I feel Norwich are a big club and I don't feel as if I have taken a step down," he added.

"I spoke to Hucks, and I even spoke to Dickson when he came off after the Newcastle game and he said how much he likes it down here and said it is a good place to play football. I think the players have made me feel as welcome as the manager did. I think they want me to join and enhance the team and enhance the squad."

Croft had been at Manchester City since the age of 12, making 32 appearances – four of those being starts – scoring one goal.

# CAPTAIN'S LOG

Adam Drury, by his own admission, has done much growing-up over the past few seasons. Three years ago everything seemed very rosy for the former Peterborough United man. As Canaries' team captain, Drury had just collected the First Division Championship trophy on the balcony of City Hall in front of thousands of adoring fans. They were scenes which would live with Drury for many years to come, and perhaps carry him through some of the darker days which were about to follow.

Promotion to the Premiership brought many new challenges for everyone at Carrow Road. A tough start saw the Canaries down at the foot of the table for the opening few months, with Drury himself suffering a loss of form. For the first time since signing from London Road for £500,000 in 2001, Drury found himself out of the team. It also meant he lost the captain's armband – another kick in the teeth if ever he needed one. By his own admission, it the toughest moment of Drury's young career.

But the player showed great character to recover from that set-back, and he found himself back in the side after Christmas, his comeback completed by his equaliser in the thrilling 4-4 draw against Middlesbrough at Carrow Road.

Since then the captain's armband has done the rounds, with the likes of Darren Huckerby, Andy Hughes, Craig Fleming and Youssef Safri all taking the responsibility at various stages last season. In short, no-one seemed capable of making the captaincy their own. Never an easy task, mind you.

But boss Nigel Worthington moved this summer to put all the uncertainty to bed and name Drury as team captain for this campaign. And the player himself said it was a different Drury to the one last time round who accepted the honour.

"It was great to be named captain again," he said.

"It's not something you say no to when you are offered it. I couldn't turn it down. I'm a bit more experienced now and far more of a senior figure than I was before. Before we had people like Iwan and Malky here, but now I'm one of those senior players."

Indeed, Malky and Iwan have long since departed with the likes of Craig Fleming heading up the senior group of players with long-term experience of playing in Norfolk. At 27 it seems strange to be describing Drury as one of the senior names, but that is most certainly the case. Drury is now most certainly one of the players the younger ones in the squad look up to and ask for advice – one of the reasons he now holds the captaincy, perhaps.

And Drury said his experiences of being a previous captain would stand him in good stead this time round. After all, what doesn't kill you only makes you stronger. Or so they say. "It's taught me a few things, that's for sure," said Drury, speaking as a man of experience. "I've learned that as a captain it's not your job to be everyone's friend the whole time."

| L | T | B | J | A | R | R | O | L | D | X | Z | K | D |
|---|---|---|---|---|---|---|---|---|---|---|---|---|---|
| F | C | R | R | J | M | T | M | Y | L | O | G | V | V |
| R | W | A | K | F | K | Y | A | G | P | B | O | B | T |
| X | G | B | N | J | K | L | L | O | Q | S | A | B | I |
| Q | T | N | Y | A | C | M | H | K | K | S | L | L | C |
| R | Y | R | I | R | R | S | J | D | M | E | M | F | K |
| R | R | L | A | L | L | Y | N | H | K | R | W | C | E |
| D | Y | B | B | E | T | K | S | C | N | P | N | F | T |
| T | G | Q | V | V | B | A | N | T | G | Y | L | C | O |
| H | U | A | F | F | M | F | W | I | O | A | J | N | F |
| K | R | N | D | T | H | K | G | P | G | R | X | T | F |
| T | Z | G | N | D | V | K | R | S | Q | G | E | W | I |
| K | T | J | F | E | R | Z | L | V | L | M | H | K | C |
| N | X | F | T | N | L | L | T | U | O | G | U | D | E |

# Carrow Road Wordsearch

Do you look upon Carrow Road as your second home? Can you find the following 12 words which relate to the Canaries' stadium? Some go sideways, some backwards, some up, some down and one is diagonal.

These are the words you are looking for:

| | | |
|---|---|---|
| PITCH | BARCLAY | JARROLD |
| TUNNEL | GOAL | FLAGS |
| DUGOUT | WATLING | PRESS BOX |
| CANARY STORE | TRAVEL SHOP | TICKET OFFICE |

*Answers are on page 61.*

# PLAYER PROFILES

**ROBERT GREEN**

A product of the Club's youth system, Robert looked set to become only the sixth Norwich City player to travel to a World Cup finals tournament this summer. However a torn groin muscle suffered in an England B match with Belarus ended his World Cup dreams and ruled-him out of the start of the Championship season. A great shot-stopper with incredible reactions, Green is also excellent in one-on-one situations. Last season he passed 200 league appearances for the Club and will be looking to push Paul Robinson for the England number one jersey in the future.

ROBERT GREEN

PAUL GALLACHER

**PAUL GALLACHER**

Paul signed for Norwich City on a free transfer from Dundee United in June 2004, but had to wait until April 2006 to make his debut for the Club, deputising for Robert Green following the England keeper's injury in warm-up at Hillsborough. Paul, a former Scottish international, responded magnificently with four outstanding displays between the posts for Norwich as the 2005-2006 season came to an end. He was rewarded for his performances with a new two-year contract at the Club in the summer.

**GARY DOHERTY**

The Doc capped an excellent campaign last season by being voted Norwich City's Player of the Year. The former Tottenham and Luton man missed just four games for the Canaries and finally cemented his place at the heart of defence after previously operating as a striker. Formidable in the air with a great ability to read the game, his commitment could never be questioned. A former Republic of Ireland international, the Doc has become somewhat of a cult hero at Carrow Road, christened "the ginger Pele" by some fans.

GARY DOHERTY

# PLAYER PROFILES

## ADAM DRURY

This former Peterborough United left-back made his 200th league appearance for Norwich in their final league match of last season, against Wolves. One of the best defenders outside of the Premiership, very few right-wingers get the better of Adam. Solid in the tackle, he is also very adept at denying his opponent the opportunity to get crosses in and is more than useful in the air, having occasionally played at centre-back.

ADAM DRURY

JURGEN COLIN

## JURGEN COLIN

Jurgen was a £250,000 signing from PSV Eindhoven in July 2005. A stylish right-back, he had previously spent all of his career at PSV with loan spells at Racing Genk (Belgium) and NAC Breda (Holland). Quick, decisive in the tackle and a good passer of the ball he was slightly reticent to break forward, but this will no doubt follow once he totally adjusts to the pace of the English game.

## CRAIG FLEMING

Craig extended his proud record of not missing a game for the Canaries to an impressive 101 games before losing his place in the team in mid-September 2005.

A tremendously consistent defender, his experience and awareness, allied to his competitive nature make him a very tough opponent. Primarily a central defender, Craig was also deployed at right-back later in the season, where he enjoyed the extra freedom to link up with his midfield and attack. Rewarded with a testimonial against Newcastle in July.

CRAIG FLEMING

DICKSON ETUHU

## DICKSON ETUHU

A £450,000 capture from Preston North End in January 2006 following a previous month-long loan spell at Carrow Road, Dickson is a powerful midfield player with all the attributes necessary to succeed in the modern game. He is at his best when breaking up opposition attacks and then moving forward with the ball at his feet. Difficult to dispossess when in possession of the ball, the Canaries will be hoping that he will find the finish to compliment some of his attacking play.

**YOUSSEF SAFRI**

Youssef made 30 league appearances for Norwich in 2005-2006 as a combination of injury and his African Cup of Nations duty for Morocco ensured that he was unable to become the dominant figure all City fans hoped he would have been. A strong and competitive midfielder with a superb range of passing skills, he has the ability to completely dictate his team's pattern of play. He combines the simple with the spectacular. His explosive shooting only brought him one goal last season, but the fans love it when he takes aim from 25 or 30 yards.

**DARREN HUCKERBY**

Darren ended the 2005-2006 season as runner-up to Gary Doherty in Norwich City's 'Player of the Year' voting. His scintillating performances on the left flank were a real highlight for the fans as he continued to make life miserable for Championship defences up and down the country. His electric pace and superb close control when in full flight, make him almost impossible to keep quiet for ninety minutes. A true Canary hero, his place in Norwich City legend was confirmed in March 2006 when he was elected to join the Club's Hall of Fame.

**ROBERT EARNSHAW**

Eight goals in 15 appearances for Norwich followed his £2.75 million transfer window move in January 2006. This diminutive Welsh international striker made an immediate impact on the Carrow Road crowd with his goal-scoring exploits and extravagant goal celebrations. Quick off the mark, he is an absolute livewire when the ball is in and around the penalty area, with his career goal-scoring record highlighting his predatory instincts. He possesses tremendously quick feet and has an ability to outwit his opponent in confined spaces.

# PLAYER PROFILES

### IAN HENDERSON

This Norfolk-born striker has graduated through the Norwich City Academy set up and up to the end of last season has 76 senior appearances to his name. A regular member of various England age group sides, up to Under-20 level, he prefers to play up front with his back to goal, where his lively running off the ball combined with his fiercely competitive nature make him a difficult player to play against.

IAN HENDERSON

ANDY HUGHES

### ANDY HUGHES

Signed from Reading for £500,000 in July 2005, Andy is a real team player whose non-stop running and enthusiasm sets a real example for his team-mates. He has the ability to fulfil a number of roles for his team, but arguably enjoyed his best games for Norwich when playing as the most forward of a five man midfield, working hard to join the lone front man, especially when this system was employed away from home.

### RYAN JARVIS

Ryan endured a difficult season with a series of niggling injuries restricting his opportunities at senior level. After forcing his way into Nigel Worthington's reckoning and scoring an excellent goal at Luton, he was forced to sit out over three months with an ankle injury. Despite these setbacks he was offered and signed, a new two-year contract with Norwich and finished the campaign back in the senior reckoning. A clever striker, in the Teddy Sheringham mould, he has great technique and the vision to create chances for others.

RYAN JARVIS

## MATTHIEU LOUIS-JEAN

This fast, accomplished right-back was hoping to make a big impact with his new employers when, after just two matches, he tore a hamstring muscle which kept him out of action for the rest of the season. This was a devastating blow for this popular Frenchman who had always played particularly well against the Canaries with his former side Nottingham Forest in the past.

## LEON McKENZIE

A big crowd favourite at Carrow Road with his non-stop running and chasing, Leon's absence from the Canaries' line-up for much of the season through a series of niggling ankle injuries did much to de-rail any hopes of a swift return to the Premiership. Powerfully built and with a direct style, Leon never allows defenders the time and space to settle. He has a good leap and likes to commit defenders by running at them with the ball and is always in and around the penalty area when chances are being created.

## PAUL McVEIGH

Paul made his 200th Norwich appearance during the 2005-2006 season which saw him finish third in the supporters' Player of the Year voting. A clever and intuitive player who has great awareness of the players and space around him, always seeming to know what to do with the ball before it even arrives at his feet. Particularly adept at creating space for himself around the edge of the penalty area to get his shots away. Enjoyed a tremendously productive spell around Christmas when playing in his preferred position as an out and out striker.

# PLAYER PROFILES

### CARL ROBINSON

A regular member of the full Welsh squad, Carl joined Norwich from Sunderland for £50,000 in January 2006 following a successful loan spell. Predominantly a holding midfield player who likes to get his foot on the ball and bring his team-mates into play with passes to feet. He has good vision and can unlock defences with one pass and although he has yet to register a goal for the Canaries he does like to break forward ahead of his strikers.

### JASON SHACKELL

Jason sustained a nasty ankle ligament injury which kept him out of action for five months last season. On his return to the side he once again displayed all the attributes that have earmarked him as one of the best young central defenders in the country. He is very strong in the air and is brave in the challenge, being prepared to get hurt in attempts to block shots on goal. He plays on the left hand side of the central defensive pairing and has the ability to pick out his strikers with long diagonal passes.

### PETER THORNE

A free transfer acquisition from Cardiff City in the summer of 2005, Peter was restricted to just 11 starts for the Canaries last season. A traditional style centre-forward, he relies on good service from the flanks to do what he does best – scoring goals, as his tally of 164 career goals would suggest. Competitive in the air and good with his back to goal he is a penalty area predator rather than the scorer of spectacular goals.

# CROSSWORD

## ACROSS

2) Norwich play in this league (12)
9) Team captain (5)
10) Nigel Worthington was previously manager at this club (9)
12) Club Captain (7)
14) Robert Earnshaw's first City goal was against this club (8)
16) City's England 'keeper (5)
18) Marked his debut with two goals against Ipswich (8)
19) City's training ground (6)
20) Player of the Year (7)

## DOWN

1) Ryan Jarvis made his Canary debut against this club (7)
3) The new first team coach (6)
4) Craig Fleming was signed from this club (6)
5) Canaries' kit manufacturer (4)
6) Signed from Sunderland last season (8)
7) Signed in the summer from Manchester City (5)
8) City's arch rivals (7)
11) They are on sale at every home game (10)
13) Canary defender born in Stevenage (8)
15) The Canaries won the Milk Cup at this stadium (7)
17) Main club sponsor (5)

***Answers are on page 61.***

# UPCOMING YOUNGSTERS

### ANDREW CAVE-BROWN

Andrew is a very versatile Scottish Under-18 international who made his Canary debut in the FA Cup Third Round tie against West Ham at Carrow Road in January 2006. He is equally at home in either full-back position, on the right-hand side of midfield and also played regularly for the youth team in the heart of defence.

ANDREW CAVE-BROWN

ROSSI JARVIS

### ROSSI JARVIS

The younger brother of Ryan, Rossi emerged from the Norwich youth system to make five senior appearances for the Canaries in season 2005-2006. Something of a utility player, he made the breakthrough playing as a competitive midfielder, but probably regards himself as a defender and it was at right-back that he made his full debut, against West Ham in the FA Cup Third Round in January 2006. Fearless in the tackle and composed when in possession he could yet develop into a regular in either defence or midfield.

### MICHAEL SPILLANE

Michael became the Club's second youngest ever FA Cup player when he made his senior debut against West Ham in January 2006. Two more first team appearances towards the end of the season gave Norwich fans a glimpse of his talents. He looked confident and assured, despite playing in the slightly unfamiliar right-back position and he will be hoping for more senior opportunities next season. Michael is able to play in many roles, but probably prefers playing in central defence where his ability to read the game and make big tackles really comes to the fore.

MICHAEL SPILLANE

JOE LEWIS

### JOE LEWIS

Standing at a towering 6ft 5in, Joe is the perfect height and build for a goalkeeper and is highly regarded by all the coaching staff at Colney. Joe signed as a professional two seasons ago but has yet to make a first team appearance. However, the teenager has seen plenty of reserve match action as he continues his development and looks to follow in the footsteps of fellow youth team product Robert Green.

# 10 AMAZING FACTS

## ABOUT ROBERT EARNSHAW

1 Robert's mother used to play semi-professional football – which might explain where he gets his goal scoring skills from!

2 Earnie was born on the outskirts of a Zambian mining town and moved to Wales when he was nine-years-old – meaning he had to learn English virtually from scratch!

3 He lived in Zambia because his English father was working as the manager of a nearby coal mine.

4 Earnie first started playing football in Wales, but it was only in his teens when he began to catch the eye, once scoring 80 goals in just one season for his school!

5 Earnie's first shot at the big time came when he was spotted playing for his school by a scout for Cardiff City's youth team.

6 In August 1997 he was awarded a one-year YTS contract with the club and eventually signed as a professional, going on to score 107 goals in 167 games before moving to West Brom for £3m in 2004.

7 His hat-trick for West Brom in March 2005 made Earnie the first player to score three goals at every level of English football, the FA Cup, League Cup and full international level.

8 Earnie has been doing his trademark front somersault goal celebration since he was very young – and he's never injured himself in the process!

9 Earnie is easy to spot around the city as he drives a giant American manufactured Hummer, one of the biggest road vehicles around!

10 However his footwear isn't quite as big – Earnie wears a size five football boot!

# STAFF PROFILES

## NIGEL WORTHINGTON

First Team Manager

Nigel was appointed Norwich City manager in January 2001 after a successful spell as caretaker boss following the resignation of Bryan Hamilton. During his time at the Club, Nigel turned the Canaries' fortunes around from a First Division outfit threatened with relegation to a side which won promotion to the Premiership as Champions in 2004. A former captain of Northern Ireland he enjoyed an excellent playing career, starting with Notts County before moving to Sheffield Wednesday – a club he played more than 400 games for.

## DOUG LIVERMORE

Assistant Manager

Doug brings a wealth of experience to the Canaries' assistant manager's role, now in his second spell with the Club after being an influential part of City's famous 71-72 promotion-winning side. A Liverpool man, he progressed through the youth ranks at Anfield and made 16 appearances for them before moving to Norwich. A long and distinguished coaching career has seen Doug working at the very highest level, including spells at both Tottenham Hotspur and Liverpool.

## KEITH WEBB

Reserve Team Manager

A former Norwich City trainee, Keith played as a centre-half in the Canaries' South East Counties League winning side of 1980. Although he was not offered a playing contract, Keith remained with the Club and was awarded the role of full-time youth team coach in 1986. Keith has played a major part in the development of talents such as Chris Sutton, Ruel Fox, Darren Eadie and Craig Bellamy. Keith has been reserve team boss since January 2001.

## NEAL REYNOLDS

Physiotherapist

Neal is a fully chartered physiotherapist and has a wealth of experience in the football world, having previously worked at West Bromwich Albion and Oxford United. Neal is the first port of call for players who are injured, and can often be seen on matchdays sprinting onto the pitch to treat players if they receive any knocks. Affectionately known as "The Fridge" at Colney, Neal is a popular character and a key member of Norwich City's backroom team.

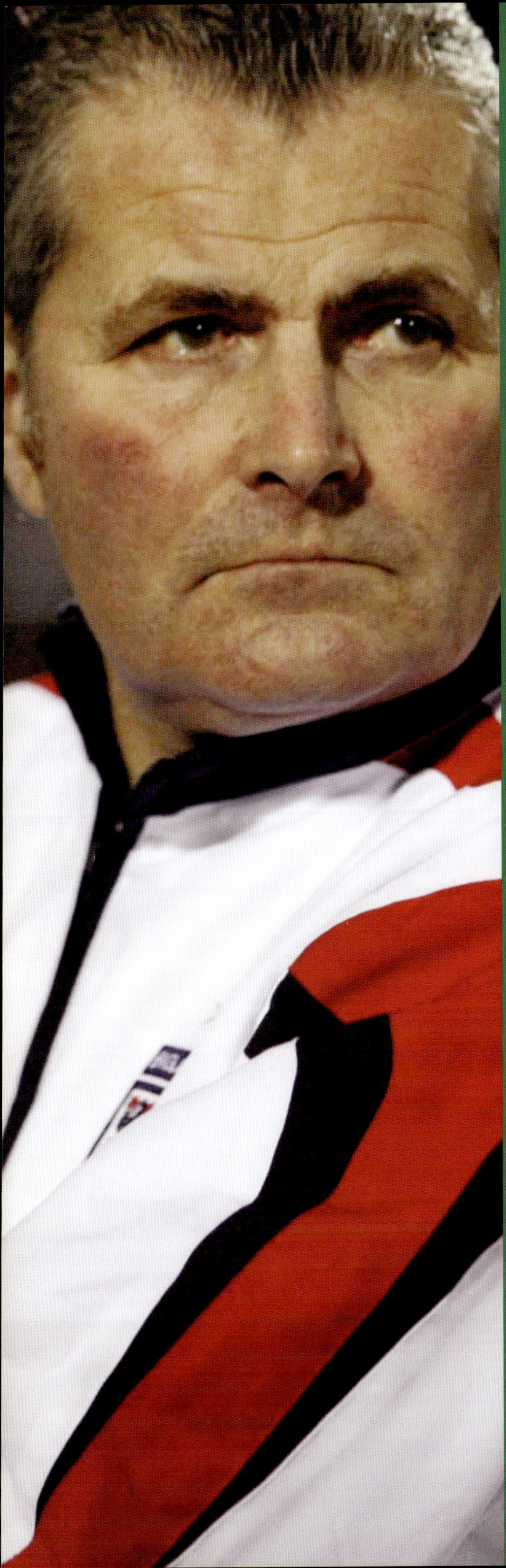

# PROFILE ON NEW COACH MARTIN HUNTER

He's worked with some of the biggest superstars in the game – and now he's at Norwich City!

Former England U19 manager Martin Hunter joined the Canaries in the summer to become their new first team coach.

Martin's main job is down on the Colney training pitches, working with the first team to ensure they are fully prepared for their next match.

An expert in coaching, Martin has worked with some of the biggest names in the game during his time as an England youth coach – including England stars Joe Cole, Michael Carrick and Theo Walcott.

And now he is using his expertise at Colney to assist boss Nigel Worthington in getting the very best out of Norwich's players.

Hunter said he had no hesitation in joining the Canaries when he was offered the chance.

"It was a fantastic opportunity for me," he said. "Norwich City is a very ambitious club and I was very impressed with the way things are run. I had two or three offers to return to club football, but this was too good an opportunity to turn down."

Hunter began his coaching career as assistant manager at Stoke and Bradford City before joining the Football Association as a youth coach 13 years ago.

He initially joined as a director of regional coaching before working his way up the ranks to work with the national under-15 and under-16 squads.

Before he joined Norwich he was working as U19 head coach, where he worked with several Norwich City stars, including Ian Henderson, Ryan Jarvis and Joe Lewis.

He holds the prestigious UEFA Pro licence and has also worked as a scout for the senior England squad.

**BACK ROW:**
Neal Reynolds (Physiotherapist), Peter Shaw (Assistant Physiotherapist) Dickson Etuhu, Jason Shackell, Matthew Halliday, Paul Gallacher (GK), Joe Lewis (GK), Robert Green (GK), Gary Doherty, Michael Spillane, Jurgen Colin, James Hollman (Goalkeeping Coach), Gavin Drake (Performance Coach)

**MIDDLE ROW:**
Terry Postle (Kit Manager), Dave Carolan (Sports Scientist), Keith Webb (Reserve Team Manager), Leon McKenzie, Rossi Jarvis, Carl Robinson, Peter Thorne, Andy Hughes, Youssef Safri, Ricky Martin (Academy Manager), David Williams (Youth Team Coach & Technical Director), Danny Young (Assistant Kit Manager)

**FRONT ROW:**
Andrew Fisk, Matthieu Louis-Jean, Paul McVeigh, Ryan Jarvis, Adam Drury, Doug Livermore (Assistant Manager), Nigel Worthington (Manager), Martin Hunter (First Team Coach), Craig Fleming, Darren Huckerby, Ian Henderson, Robert Earnshaw, Robert Eagle

*Note – Andrew Cave-Brown absent due to international commitments.*

Norwich City
Football Club

INTERVIEW WITH

# DARREN HUCKERBY

***ONE of the most exciting players to pull on a Norwich City shirt, Darren Huckerby is the type of footballer who gets fans on the edge of their seats.***

Whether playing up front as a striker or down the left as a winger, Huckerby's pace and dribbling ability sends shivers down the necks of Championship defenders.

A scorer of spectacular goals, as well as a creator, Huckerby is loved by fans for his direct style and never-say-die approach.

Hucks even earned himself a place in Norwich City's Hall of Fame last season, although the 30-year-old admitted the honour had come as a great surprise to him.

"It was pretty unexpected to be honest," he said. "It's come so soon in my time at the Club. It's fans' votes as well, which means a lot to me. Obviously I've had a couple of successful seasons here so it's nice to mark it with this honour.

"It's nice to know the supporters think that much of you. I've worked hard since coming here and I've had a lot of happy times with the Club."

Huckerby arrived at Carrow Road on a full-time basis in a blaze of glory on Boxing Day 2003. The former Manchester City man had spent a hugely successful three months on loan and stolen the hearts of Canaries' fans in the process as he helped propel City from mid-table mediocrity to the top of the division.

And Hucks agreed that his arrival on a full-time basis signalled a new era for Norwich City and demonstrated the Club's ambition to return to the Premiership.

## DARREN HUCKERBY FACTFILE

| | |
|---|---|
| NAME: | Darren Huckerby |
| DATE OF BIRTH: | 23/04/76 |
| BIRTHPLACE: | Nottingham |
| HEIGHT: | 5ft 11in |
| WEIGHT: | 12st (76kg) |
| PREVIOUS CLUBS: | Lincoln City, Newcastle United, Millwall (loan), Coventry City, Leeds United, Manchester City, Nottingham Forrest (loan), Norwich City. |
| CANARIES' DEBUT: | September 13, 2003 v Burnley (H) 2-0 |

"I think so," he said. "I can't remember exactly, but I think we were in 13th position when I joined, along with Peter Crouch and Kevin Harper. That really seemed to kick-start things straight away and we never really looked back."

And Hucks said there was no avoiding the clamour for him to stay in Norfolk, with supporters making it pretty clear they wanted the player to make the move from Manchester City.

"I had an idea of all the pressure off the pitch about people wanting me to stay," he said.

"They made it pretty clear they wanted me to stay. I wanted to stay too and it was quite a saga to make it happen. It looked like I was going back to Manchester City for a while and it was a difficult spell for me.

"It was even more difficult because my wife and kids were away from me and that didn't make it easy. But we managed to get through it and I did my best to make the proper decision. In the end, there wasn't a decision to make. I wanted to come."

Bringing Huckerby to Carrow Road was seen as a calculated gamble by the Board of Norwich City. But it paid off as Norwich returned to the Premiership as First Division Champions.

"Obviously it was a big step for the Club in bringing me in," he said. "It sent a message out to the rest of the league that we meant business. From there we've gone and bought Dean Ashton for £3m and now Robert Earnshaw for a similar amount. That shows how far the Club has come in such a short space of time."

And Huckerby said winning the Championship with Norwich ranked as one of the biggest highlights of his career.

"Definitely," he said. "I've been successful before in my career at other clubs. When we won it at Manchester City everyone knew we were going to do it. We were favourites and had an expensive squad full of top players. But when I came to Norwich it was different. Other clubs didn't realise how good we were until it was too late. By the time they realised we were in a very good position and couldn't be stopped. For Norwich to win the Championship remains a massive achievement for the football club."

# *NORWICH CITY'S ACADEMY – Producing the stars of tomorrow!*

THE Canaries have a rich history of producing some of the most talented players in the game.

Chris Sutton, Craig Bellamy, Ruel Fox, Darren Eadie, Ade Akinbiyi, Danny Mills and Robert Green all began their careers as youngsters with Norwich City.

And the Academy continues to turn out stars of tomorrow, with Jason Shackell making a name for himself in the first team and the likes of Michael Spillane, Rossi Jarvis and Joe Lewis rising through the ranks.

And the dedicated team of Academy coaches – led by manager Ricky Martin – continues to work tirelessly around the clock to discover the next potential superstar.

Working alongside Ricky, Academy technical director Dave Williams knows how to spot a good young footballer.

Dave is a former Norwich City midfielder and after retiring from the game went on to work with Manchester United's highly-regarded youth side, helping develop players such as David Beckham and Gary Neville.

So it looks as though Norwich City's future is in very good hands!

# THE TACTIC ZONE

***The Academy facilities at Colney are often the envy of rival clubs, both at Championship and Premiership level.***

And a fundraising initiative has now been launched to move the Academy facilities up to the next level, giving the Canaries an even greater advantage at youth football level.

The Tactic Zone appeal was launched in February 2006 with the aim of raising £250,000 to build a new state-of-the-art off-field facility at the training ground.

The new building will give coaches a place to teach players the tactical side of the game, an element becoming more and more important in the development of young footballers.

Heading-up the fundraising drive is former Canary midfield star Jeremy Goss, himself a product of the Club's youth system.

The hero of the UEFA win over Bayern Munich in 1993 said the fundraising had got off to a great start and appealed to local businesses and groups to get right behind it.

"I think it's vital because the concept of the Academy is that youngsters from the local community are given the chance to progress and reach their goal of becoming professional footballers," he said.

"If we have this new building in place it would make a big difference. At the moment youngsters are being taught in the canteen at Colney, and this isn't acceptable. We need this area.

"It will help players with their off-field development and will hopefully assist the Club in developing its first team stars of the future."

THE ACADEMY

TZ

TACTIC ZONE

SECURING THE FUTURE

***"...the concept of the Academy is that youngsters from the local community are given the chance to progress and reach their goal of becoming professional footballers..."***

INTERVIEW WITH

# JASON SHACKELL

***A PRIME example of how the Academy can bear fruit, young defender Jason Shackell is now making a name for himself in the Canaries' first team.***

Born in Stevenage, Shackell was snapped-up by City scouts at a young age and rose up through the youth ranks before making his senior debut in 2001 away at Derby County.

Since then, Shackell has gone on to become a first team regular and was a key figure in the Canaries fight against relegation from the Premiership two seasons ago.

But his career came to a standstill last season when he suffered ankle ligament damage in a reserve match against Watford at Carrow Road.

It was an injury which ruled Shackell out of most of the season. The 23-year-old bounced back well, but admitted it had been a difficult time in his career.

"It was the first serious injury of my career," he said. "When it happened I didn't really know what was going on. I just fell and landed really awkwardly. It was my first serious injury and, fingers crossed, it will be my last."

Shackell's football education at Carrow Road has been a swift one. Two seasons ago he went from being a regular reserve team member to marking the likes of Wayne Rooney and Didier Drogba in the Premiership.

They were tests he passed with flying colours, and Shackell said playing against the best had been a good learning curve for him.

"It was a massive experience for me," he said. "You find yourself playing against some of the best players in the world all of a sudden. And they all offered different challenges.

"One week you're up against Drogba, who is strong and experienced. The next you're facing Kevin Davies, who's your traditional target man. Then

there's Wayne Rooney. They are all world class players and they all offered different challenges.

"They are all good strikers," he said. "It was a great experience for me. You are playing against the best strikers in the league and they are the players you have grown-up watching on television. They are the players you want to be up against.

"I've learnt so much at Norwich City – particularly playing alongside people like Craig Fleming and Gary Doherty."

# Quiz Time – Spot the ball

## Funny Faces

***Can you spot the three City players in each of our four funny faces?***

A

B

C

D

## Spot the Difference

*There are 9 minor differences between these two pictures. Can you find them all?*

## Captain's Quiz

***Can you answer Captain Canary's 10 trivia questions?***

1. From which club did the Canaries sign striker Robert Earnshaw?
2. Which Canary enjoyed a testimonial match against Newcastle United in July 2006?
3. What nationality is defender Matthieu Louis-Jean?
4. Carl Robinson began is career with which Championship club?
5. Goalkeeper Paul Gallacher was signed from which Scottish club?
6. Who was the Canaries' Player of the Year in 2005-06?
7. Which company sponsor the Community Stand at Carrow Road?
8. Which player joined the Canaries in the 2006 January transfer window from Preston North End?
9. Which company manufacture the Canaries' kit?
10. Who was the last Norwich City player to play for England?

*Answers on page 61.*

# LEON McKENZIE ON MANCHESTER UNITED WIN

***IT was one of the highlights of Norwich's Premiership season – and a game which triggered the run which almost saved City's top-flight skins.***

In the end, a 6-0 defeat at Fulham on the final day of the season saw the Canaries relegated.

But not before they had humiliated star-studded Manchester United at Carrow Road.

The date was April 9, 2005. The Red Devils had come to Carrow Road looking to close the gap on champions-elect Chelsea with a comfortable win.

With an FA Cup semi-final against Newcastle just days away, United manager Sir Alex Ferguson chose to rest some of his star names, leaving the likes of Wayne Rooney, Christiano Ronaldo and Ruud Van Nistelrooy on the subs' bench.

With City on a miserable five-game losing streak and stranded at the foot of the Premiership, few would have bet against the under-strength visitors from claiming the three points.

But City were in no mood to simply roll over, and produced one of the gutsiest displays of the season to record a comfortable 2-0 win over United.

And it was City star Leon McKenzie who wrapped-up the win for Norwich in the 66th minute, following up Dean Ashton's headed opener early in the second half.

For McKenzie, the game still ranks as one of the highlights of his career. And scoring against a team like Manchester United was what he'd always dreamed of doing as a youngster.

"It means so much to me because of where I've come from," he said. "It was a game which all the boys wanted to do well in and to get that goal meant I was now scoring against the very best in the game.

"I always dreamt of scoring against teams like Manchester United when I was growing up. It just

# LEON McKENZIE ON ANTI-BULLYING

LEON McKenzie takes no nonsense from defenders, but the City striker had to learn to stand-up for himself from a young age. McKenzie was bullied as a child at school and knows all about the heartache and misery caused to victims.

The former Peterborough man turned to boxing to learn to defend himself, but the livewire forward is now helping other children overcome the threat of bullies. Last season he backed Norfolk County Council's Anti-Bullying Week campaign and said bullying had to be stamped out.

"I was bullied at school when I was a kid and that's when I turned to boxing. Bullying is something that I hate, it can cause a lot of suffering. Often the bullies need help too. There can be things going on in their life, problems at home for example, which they need help with.

"This is a great campaign and it's great for people to get behind it. I've got kids of my own and I would hate the idea that they were being bullied. No one wants their children to be bullied, which is why this anti-bullying campaign is so important."

goes to show what you can accomplish – look at what Peter Crouch has achieved. He's played in the World Cup."

With Sir Alex throwing on Rooney, Ronaldo and Van Nistelrooy to salvage something from the game, Norwich knew their 1-0 lead was a slender one.

So when McKenzie hit the back of the net, Canary fans could begin to dream.

"I still remember the goal really well," said McKenzie. "I remember Dean Ashton breaking down the left and I thought to myself, I'm going to get in the box to give myself a chance.

"He dinked the ball across to me and I had to make sure I kept the ball under control, because it's very easy to blast them over the bar. But when it hit the net you could see what it meant to me by the way I celebrated."

McKenzie's celebration earned himself a booking, with his shirt coming off in front of a jubilant Norwich and Peterborough Stand. Not that he cared.

"When you're in a situation like that you've got to just enjoy the moment," he said. "I'll always remember it as one of the highlights of my career."

INTERVIEW WITH

# JAKE HUMPHREY

He's a familiar face on CBBC – but he's also a familiar face at Carrow Road! Television presenter Jake Humphrey has been a Norwich City fan for most of his life and still comes back to Norfolk to watch his favourite side in action whenever he can.

And Jake, who can be seen on children's sports programme Sportsround, said he'd been following City for quite some time.

"I first used to watch City when Dave Stringer was manager and Ian Butterworth was captain," he said. "I would go with my mate James and we would sit in the family enclosure in what is now the Jarrold Stand. I have fond memories of the chip shop outside the ground which is now a house! How times change!"

Jake's high-flying television career means he can't get back to see as many games as he would like at Carrow Road.

"I try to get back as much as possible," he said. "If I can't make it to a game I make sure I mention City on the telly as much as possible so there is no question as to who I support!

"I currently present Sportsround, which I love – but it is live at 11.45am every Saturday so I find it hard to get back to Norwich for 3pm.

"I try to get to as many London games as possible, but our away form has been so poor the last couple of seasons it's proved a pretty tough time for us away fans!"

Jake's career means he mixes in some pretty exclusive circles, and he said he occasionally bumped into celebrity City fans – and tried to convert others!

"Obviously I know Simon Thomas who was once on Blue Peter and is a fellow City fan," he said. "We normally discuss the games via text message.

"Chris Moyles is a big Leeds fan and I always tell him how much better City are! Most people seem to know who I support so when we get guests on the show they like to discuss it and most people think Norwich are a great team who like to play great football.

"I love coming back and meeting the fans. I think they really like the fact I big-up the Club as much as possible. They always ask me about life at CBBC and ask what I think about the team – and I'm always honest!"

Jake used to hero worship the likes of Jeremy Goss from the stands when he'd watch the team as a youngster and admitted he was often in awe of the players.

"I also worshipped Ruel Fox and Chris Sutton and once saw Bryan Gunn in our local pub and was totally star-struck – he seemed massive!"

Jake likes to sit in the Barclay whenever possible and said he loved being at Carrow Road on a matchday.

"I really love Carrow Road, obviously, as it's my Club. But I also think the ground has a great atmosphere and is definitely good enough for the Premiership. Everyone in Norwich should be proud of our fantastic ground and the brilliant way the club is run."

Jake is a big fan of striker Robert Earnshaw but said there was one player in particular he'd love to see at Norwich City – if only they had enough money!

"No doubt – Ronaldinho. He has to be the world's best player and I think he would enjoy life in Norfolk, sailing the Broads every weekend! Him or Thierry Henry and Earnie up front would be great!"

# soccerPM!

***NIGHT time matches at Carrow Road are always special occasions. Even at reserve team level.***

The Club's Soccer PM initiative has been a huge success over the past two seasons, with thousands of youngsters taking advantage of the great range of activities and events available on reserve team nights at Carrow Road.

First team players including Robert Green, Jason Shackell, Andy Hughes, Ryan Jarvis and Paul Gallacher have all given up their spare time to sign autographs in the Russell Allison Lounge beneath The Barclay Stand on Soccer PM nights.

Crowds of up to 6,000 turned up for games against Chelsea and Arsenal's reserve team sides last season. For some of the younger fans, it was their first taste of live football.

At half-time a crossbar challenge was held to see if fans could strike the bar with a football. The winners received an NCFC football signed by the entire first team! The speed kick events in the Russell Allison lounge were also very popular, with children finding out whether they had a shot as powerful as Youssef Safri!

Face painting also took place before games, with kids and their parents able to support their team by showing their true colours!

And it wasn't just the footballers on the pitch showing off their ball skills, with youngsters taught how to juggle and stilt walk with the Circus Workshop.

All in all, the Soccer PM nights have been a huge success – we look forward to seeing you at the next one!

# CAPTAIN'S GANG & TEAM CANARY

## *At Norwich City, we believe live football should be enjoyed by all ages. And we are extremely lucky to have a loyal band of young fans.*

*Many are members of Captain's Gang and Team Canary, an exclusive group for young Norwich City fans.*

*Under 12s can join Captain's Gang and take part in a host of activities laid on especially for them. Those aged between 12 and 16 can join Team Canary and be entertained by special events dedicated to their age group.*

*Captain's Gang and Team Canary members will get special cards from the Club on their birthday and be invited to the Christmas party held each year.*

*There are also special discounts for match tickets, with all members of Captain's Gang and Team Canary getting five per cent off items in the Canary Store.*

*For more information about joining Captain's Gang and Team Canary, call 0870 444 1902.*

team canary

CAPTAIN'S GANG

# McVEIGH IS READING CHAMPION

***HE'S Norwich City's pocket rocket and a firm favourite with supporters. But Paul McVeigh has much more than a footballing brain to offer.***

The Northern Irishman has led his support to a Canaries initiative to encourage more youngsters to read books.

Backed by the Club's Study Support Centre and Norfolk County Council, hundreds of school children have discovered the delights of reading at Carrow Road thanks to the scheme.

Paul's favourite book is Bill Bryson's A Short History of Everything, and felt it was important people such as himself set a good example for others.

"If they see footballers like myself reading then it is going to encourage these children," he said.

"Football is a great avenue to get children to read."

And Paul admitted his parents always encouraged him to read as a child and was glad now that they did.

"My mum was always telling me to read when I was young so I used to read Enid Blyton's Secret Seven."

***Other Norwich City players favourite children's books:***

*JASON SHACKELL – STIG OF THE DUMP*

*GARY DOHERTY – MOLLY MOON*

*CRAIG FLEMING – DANNY THE CHAMPION OF THE WORLD*

*DARREN HUCKERBY – TOM'S MIDNIGHT GARDEN*

*JOE LEWIS – THE HARRY POTTER SERIES*

DICKSON ETUHU

# YOUSSEF SAFRI

# MYSTERY PLAYER

I JOINED THE CANARIES IN MARCH 2001

I PLAY IN DEFENCE BUT LIKE TO GET FORWARD

I WAS PREVIOUSLY PLAYING FOR PETERBOROUGH UNITED

I SCORED MY FIRST GOAL FOR THE CANARIES AGAINST STOKE CITY

I WAS TEAM CAPTAIN DURING THE 2003-04 CHAMPIONSHIP-WINNING SEASON

I HAVE NOW PLAYED OVER 200 LEAGUE GAMES FOR THE CLUB

WHO AM I?

*Answers on page 61.*

# TOP 10 GOALS OF THE SEASON

### ROBERT EARNSHAW V CARDIFF (A) – APRIL 22, 2006

Robert Earnshaw returned to former club Cardiff for the first time since leaving them for West Brom back in January 2005 and was given a hero's welcome. And he ensured the return to Ninian Park was a happy one for him as he scored a spectacular winning goal to earn the Canaries' first away win of the calendar year. Andy Hughes collected a loose ball and headed into Earnshaw's path just inside the box, and he let fly with a sweet half-volley which arrowed into the top corner of the net.

### DARREN HUCKERBY V IPSWICH TOWN (A) – SEPTEMBER 18, 2005

City arrived at Portman Road looking for their first away win in more than a season. And they broke their duck in the best way possible, defeating their local rivals 1-0 in an action-packed game. Darren Huckerby had been surprisingly left on the bench for the match, but at half time he was let loose on 10-man Town and announced his arrival in some style. Gary Doherty's long ball from the back caught Town 'keeper Lewis Price in no-man's land, and Huckerby showed a cool head to round the stranded stopper and slot home.

### YOUSSEF SAFRI V HULL CITY (H) – SEPTEMBER 27, 2005

This 2-1 win was inspired by a man-of-the-match performance by Youssef Safri, and it was only right the Moroccan international made his mark with a typical thunderbolt. Norwich had gone behind to an early header from Leon Cort. But 15 minutes into the first half Safri caught the visiting defence napping as he latched onto a short corner taken by Darren Huckerby. With the City fans crying out for him to "shoot", Safri let-rip with a 20-yard scorcher which fizzed past 'keeper Myhill before he could move.

### IAN HENDERSON V BRIGHTON (A) – OCTOBER 1, 2005

City were winning 2-1 going into the last 10 minutes of this match, although it was the home side putting on the pressure to grab what would have been an unlikely point. But with the clock counting down, substitute Ian Henderson clinched a crucial third for the Canaries to put the result beyond doubt. The Academy product picked up the ball wide on the right before beating his man and cutting into the box. From the corner of the area, he bent a delightful left-foot shot into the top corner to seal the win.

### ROBERT EARNSHAW V BRIGHTON (H) – FEBRUARY 14, 2005

Norwich were 1-0 up but hanging on for all three points at home to relegation-haunted Brighton when Robert Earnshaw picked the perfect moment to register his first goal for the Canaries. The move was triggered when Robert Green showed great handling to clutch a free-kick out of the sky. He showed real awareness to throw the ball out to Darren Huckerby, who was lurking by the half-way line. His pace took him past the last man and into the box, and he unselfishly rolled the ball along the six-yard box for Earnshaw to thrash into the net and begin his trademark somersault celebration. A great move.

#### DEAN ASHTON V CRYSTAL PALACE (H) – AUGUST 13, 2005

The Canaries came face-to-face with fellow relegated side Palace at Carrow Road looking for their first win of the season. Again, they were held to a draw. Although Dean Ashton had got them off to a great start inside six minutes. Andy Hughes showed great awareness to bring the ball down before lifting an inch-perfect cross to the far post for the England U21 international. He wasted no time in side-footing a perfect volley past Gabor Kiraly and into the net via the underside of the crossbar. It was a typically clinical Ashton finish and his second of the season.

#### DARREN HUCKERBY V DERBY COUNTY (H) – FEBRUARY 18, 2006

City were coasting to a 1-0 win against managerless Derby at Carrow Road when Darren Huckerby settled the points with a spectacular shot in the 84th minute. Huckerby started the move, collecting the ball on the left and sprinting towards the edge of the visitors' box. He sprayed the ball out to McVeigh on the left, who took a touch before returning it to Huckerby 20-yards from goal. And he sent in a first time shot with his right foot which arrowed into the top corner to secure another three points at home.

#### PAUL MCVEIGH V SHEFFIELD UNITED (A) – DECEMBER 26, 2005

Sheffield United were flying high in second place in the Championship table and had yet to lose a match at home during the course of the season. The Canaries changed all that with a 3-1 win, sparked by a terrific move and finish by Paul McVeigh. City were trailing to a header by Phil Jagielka midway through the first half when McVeigh struck. The move was the result of a swift break from defence, which saw Carl Robinson head a delightful ball into McVeigh's path as he broke from midfield. He took one touch before producing an inch-perfect finish inside Paddy Kenny's far post.

#### JONATAN JOHANSSON V STOKE CITY (H) – MARCH 4, 2006

It may not have been the most spectacular goal of the season, but it was certainly one of the most dramatic. City were drawing 1-1 with Stoke with the seconds counting down when Robert Green produced a world-class save from Bangoura to secure what looked to be a disappointing draw. But 30 seconds later and Norwich had the ball in the net at the other end to grab a dramatic win. McVeigh's slide-rule pass fell perfectly into the stride of Jonatan Johansson. His nimble footwork wrong-footed 'keeper Steve Simonsen before flicking the ball home with the coolest of finishes.

#### DARREN HUCKERBY V PLYMOUTH ARGYLE (A) – JANUARY 14, 2006

A goal which only the likes of Darren Huckerby can score. There looked to be little danger when the City forward collected the ball wide on the left. But he jinked to the by-line past two defenders before lifting a shot over the head of the goalkeeper to cancel out a first half own-goal by Simon Charlton. It was a finish from the acutest of angles and again proved how Huckerby is adept at creating a chance out of nothing.

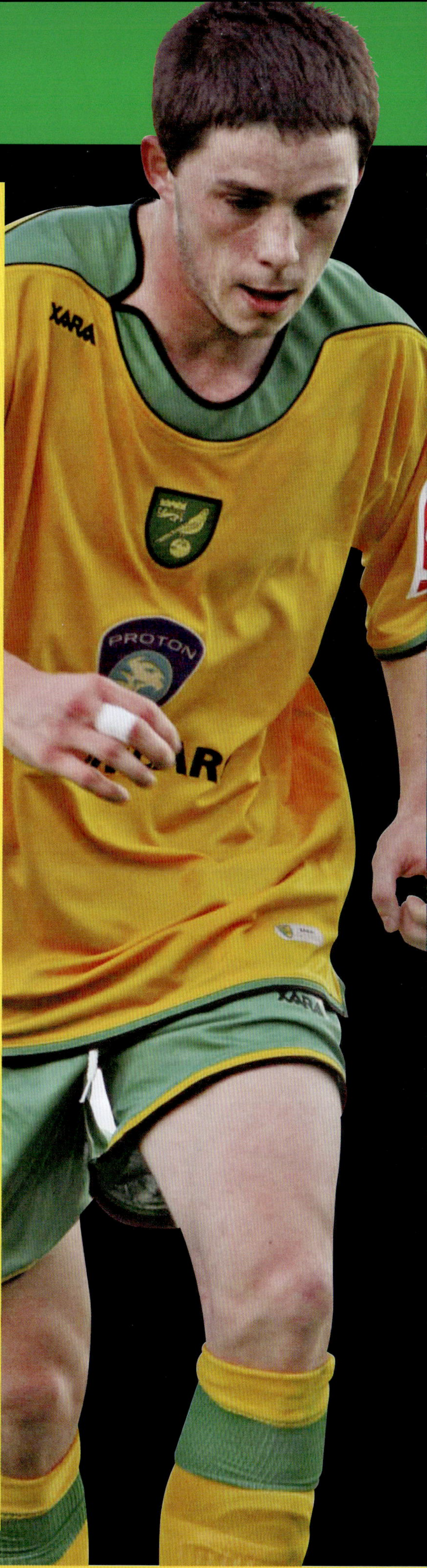

# NORWICH CITY DREAM

***We spoke to eleven Norwich City first team players and asked them to pick out a Canaries dream team – a side you would choose if time and money were no object.***

The results were certainly interesting. But we can only wonder how such a side, with all the players at their peak, would have got on in the Championship!

GOALKEEPER – ANDY GORAM

DEFENDER – CAFU

DEFENDER – FRANCO BARESI

DEFENDER – MARCEL DESAILLY

MIDFIELDER – LOTHAR MATTHAEUS

MIDFIELDER – PAUL GASCOIGNE

MIDFIELDER – PATRICK VIEIRA

STRIKER – DIEGO MARADONA

STRIKER – PELE

# TEAM

DEFENDER – PAULO MALDINI

MIDFIELDER – RYAN GIGGS

**GOALKEEPER – ANDY GORAM**

Picked by Paul Gallacher: "Growing up in Scotland I thought he was the most consistent goalkeeper and has had a great career."

**DEFENDER – FRANCO BARESI**

Picked by Craig Fleming: "He was probably the greatest defender I'd ever had the privilege of seeing. Unbelievable."

**DEFENDER – PAULO MALDINI**

Picked by Adam Drury: "He's a legend who's pretty much won everything there is to win in the game."

**DEFENDER – MARCEL DESAILLY**

Picked by Jason Shackell: "He was a great all-round defender and a World Cup winner too."

**DEFENDER – CAFU**

Picked by Jurgen Colin: "A brilliant right-back. So much quality still, despite his age."

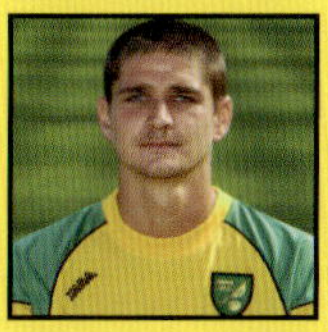

**MIDFIELDER – LOTHAR MATTHAEUS**

Picked by Carl Robinson: "A great engine and had a real commanding presence over his team, both at national and club level."

**MIDFIELDER – RYAN GIGGS**

Picked by Darren Huckerby: "An incredible player who's won almost everything and is still playing at the very top today."

**MIDFIELDER – PATRICK VIEIRA**

Picked by Dickson Etuhu: "A massive player when he was at Arsenal and probably the complete midfielder."

**MIDFIELDER – PAUL GASCOIGNE**

Picked by Paul McVeigh: "Undoubtedly the best player of his generation before it all went wrong for him."

**STRIKER – DIEGO MARADONA**

Picked by Robert Earnshaw: "Quite simply one of the best players the world has ever seen."

**STRIKER – PELE**

Picked by Leon McKenzie: "I always looked up to Ian Wright as a youngster, but for sheer skill it has to be Pele."

ROBERT EARNSHAW

# Quiz Answers

### Captain's Quiz

1. West Bromwich Albion
2. Craig Fleming
3. French
4. Wolverhampton Wanderers
5. Dundee United
6. Gary Doherty
7. Norwich Union
8. Dickson Etuhu
9. Xara
10. Robert Green

### Funny Faces

A Neck and mouth – Jason Shackell
Nose and eyes – Carl Robinson
Hair – Robert Green

B Neck and mouth – Ian Henderson
Nose and eyes – Paul Gallacher
Hair – Adam Drury

C Neck and mouth – Ryan Jarvis
Nose and eyes – Andy Hughes
Hair – Peter Thorne

D Neck and mouth – Leon McKenzie
Nose and eyes – Robert Earnshaw
Hair – Matthieu Louis-Jean

### Mystery Player

Adam Drury

### Spot the Ball

### Spot the Difference

### Carrow Road Wordsearch

### Crossword

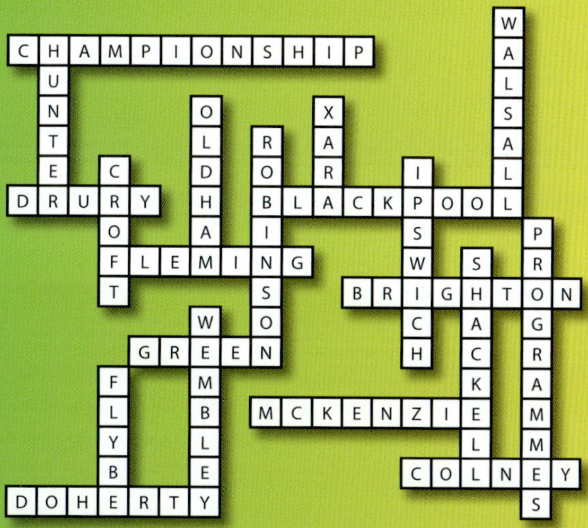

## NORWICH CITY FOOTBALL CLUB

# PHOTOCALL 2006-07

**BACK ROW:**
Neal Reynolds (Physiotherapist), Peter Shaw (Assistant Physiotherapist) Dickson Etuhu, Jason Shackell, Matthew Halliday, Paul Gallacher (GK), Joe Lewis (GK), Robert Green (GK), Gary Doherty, Michael Spillane, Jurgen Colin, James Hollman (Goalkeeping Coach), Gavin Drake (Performance Coach)

**MIDDLE ROW:**
Terry Postle (Kit Manager), Dave Carolan (Sports Scientist), Keith Webb (Reserve Team Manager), Leon McKenzie, Rossi Jarvis, Carl Robinson, Peter Thorne, Andy Hughes, Youssef Safri, Ricky Martin (Academy Manager), David Williams (Youth Team Coach & Technical Director), Danny Young (Assistant Kit Manager)

**FRONT ROW:**
Andrew Fisk, Matthieu Louis-Jean, Paul McVeigh, Ryan Jarvis, Adam Drury, Doug Livermore (Assistant Manager), Nigel Worthington (Manager), Martin Hunter (First Team Coach), Craig Fleming, Darren Huckerby, Ian Henderson, Robert Earnshaw, Robert Eagle

*Note – Andrew Cave-Brown absent due to international commitments.*